Hovering Across Time

affirmations in a complex world

Royce Holladay

Haiku and affirmations inspired by
dynamics of human interactions.

Gold Canyon Press

Hovering Across Time:
Affirmations in a Complex World

Gold Canyon Press
P.O. Box 2223
Apache Junction, Arizona 85217-2223
U.S.A.

www.goldcanyonpress.com

PB ISBN: 978-0-9821112-4-6
PRINTED IN THE UNITED STATES OF AMERICA

Also by Royce Holladay

Legacy:
Sustainability in a Complex Human System

Co-authored with Kristine Quade

Influencing Patterns for Change:
A Human Systems Dynamics Primer for Leaders

Dynamical Leadership:
Building Adaptive Capacity for Uncertain Times

Co-authored with Mallary Tytel

Simple Rules: Radical Inquiry into Self

CONTENTS

Section 1.   1
    Celebrating Community

Section 2.   17
    Connecting with Others

Section 3.   31
    Finding my Path

Section 4.   47
    Knowing Life's Beauty

Section 5.   61
    Learning My Strength

Section 6.   73
    Living and Playing

Section 7.   81
    Seeing Tomorrow's Promise

Section 8.   93
    Seeking Wisdom

Acknowledgments

A number of people contributed to the creation of this book.

- My mother, Ruth Holladay, taught me to know that words could both tell a story and paint a picture.
- My sister, Leslie Patterson, encourages and seeks the writer that is in my soul.
- Another sister, Glenda Eoyang, helps me understand the conditions of my life.
- My youngest sister, Jo Klemm, shares words with me from sources I would never have found alone.

In addition, friends have come into my life at just the right moments to teach me what I need to know, to hold my hand through difficulties and pain, to celebrate wonders and joys, and to sit quietly with me in the evening light. Thanks to each of you for your very special gifts and love.

Finally, I dedicate this book to my daughters, Toni Martinez and Tori Chandler. The lights they shine in my life are gifts that allow me to see my world in new and exciting ways. Thank you both, and I can only hope this reflects some of what you've each taught me.

Introduction

Dragonflies--changeless,
Beautiful, immutable--
Hovering across time.

I have always been drawn to dragonflies. For obvious reasons: their beauty, grace, and amazing patterns of flight delighted me as a child. As I grew older, I came to appreciate the physics that allows them to fly as they do, as well as the amazing story of their adaptation across the millennia.

There is something in a dragonfly's natural code that makes it sensitive to its surroundings, responsive to changes it encounters, and strong enough to continue to grow and reproduce in the face of tremendous change.

I have always been drawn to haiku, as well. I read somewhere about earliest haiku being written by priests who went into nature, opened themselves to the beauty around them, and wrote about the first images they saw.

When I started writing this haiku, I sometimes sat outside and observed what was around me. Other times I closed my eyes and wrote from memories--people, places, experiences. Either way, I wrote of the images that came to me--both of nature and of human interactions.

Then, I borrowed metaphors from human systems dynamics to think about individual and personal adaptation. The idea of the dragonfly stayed with me--drawing me into the rich images and curious comparisons and distinctions I tried to capture here.

I hope you enjoy my haiku for the images and memories it conjures for you--and that you can use the affirmations in your own evolving life of constant change and adaptation. Whatever you find in these pages, I thank you for your attention and hope you find it useful.

Section 1:

Celebrating Community

As one, birds take off.

Swirling and flying, each heart

Beats the flock's rhythm.

I connect to my community.
We move forward together.

One furred head comes up.

Others, smelling the danger,

Circle to protect.

I help keep my community safe.

Strong, self-sufficient—

Each member of the wild pride

Depends on others.

Others can depend on me,
and I ask for help when I need it.

Leaf's net of soft veins

Echoes the life-giving form--

The tree's stand of strength.

What gives me strength is
mirrored in my community.

The voice of the wind,

Relentless in its pursuit,

Whines at locked windows.

*In community, I am safe
from the world.*

Touch and sound connect.

Acts guided by shared knowing--

Our boundaries hold strong.

*I contribute to the community
as I reach out to others.*

Trees repeat their forms.

Life in trunk, limb, branch, and twig;

Strength in a fractal.

I mirror the strength of my community.

Each playing a part

In the community's path,

Creating shared lives.

I contribute with others
to the wholeness we share.

Drinking shared water,

Each group chooses its own time--

Guarded common space.

We recognize and accommodate
our differences.

Nature's efficient.

What one leaves, another takes—

Symbiotic lives.

We share in the health of the whole.

Strangers together,

As one to the task at hand,

They create their world.

I work with others to build community.

Teaching the children

Grounds them in our shared culture.

Our heritage stands.

*We sustain the power
of our community.*

Starling sits alone;

Quiet, watchful--others join.

Music splits the air.

*I find harmony in
our work together.*

Section 2:

Connecting with Others

Voice calls across fields--

Rounded, lonely tones of grief.

Dove calls for her mate.

I listen to others to
know their needs.

Sun bouncing off waves

Splits in a million rainbows.

I'm bathed in color.

Others' love surrounds
me in light.

Coming to the edge,

I feel the wind at my back.

Your hand steadies me.

I know others are with me
when I face great challenges.

The song, one low note,

Alone, then more voices join--

A chorus of joy.

There is joy in sharing with others.

Eagle, flying low,

Captures shining, leaping fish

To feed her family.

*I take care of those
who depend on me.*

Riches on water;

Setting sun's dying rays--

Gold, just before dark.

Knowing the bounty of life,
I celebrate fleeting gifts.

The strength that I feel...

Sunlight pulling its flowers

Toward a gentle kiss.

*I bring good to my own life
and to others.*

Sounds of your laughter,

The teasing, living, loving--

Bring peace to my soul.

I share the joy
I find in others.

Moonlight splits the dark

Sharing sun's light as its own--

Orb of reflection.

When I share with another,
neither of us is diminished.

Bark flies as limbs shake.

Squirrels play chase in the cool fall air.

Last of summer's fun.

Sometimes play is the answer,
whatever the question.

The crowd talks and laughs.

People sharing their stories.

I stand alone.

*I watch and learn
from others.*

I try to tell you

The power I feel in your arms.

Winds blow away words.

*I find ways to express
what I need to share.*

Section 3:

Finding My Path

Wild geese, sensing spring,

Drawn home by a common need,

Graceful arrows north.

*I listen to my heart to
find my dreams.*

Gnarled oak, lightning struck--

Slight sprig of green emerging.

Life will continue.

*I know endings are merely clearings
for whatever is next.*

Colors of cold steel...

The waves are rocking my boat.

It's my safe harbor.

*I know where to find
safety in my life.*

Back to childhood's home,

Pain and memories grown pale

As winter's shadows.

Who I am is stronger
because of my yesterdays.

My dreams are fragile.

Like bubbles of hope, they

Burst on rough edges.

I protect my dreams,
working to make them real.

Mirrors of my soul,

Shadowy dreams are my guides.

I am becoming.

*I work toward my dreams
to find myself.*

The dark, furrowed ground

Receives the seeds it's given,

Pushing forth new life.

*I plant new ideas, knowing
they will grow over time.*

Bright, colored pictures--

Choices are within my grasp,

Painting future's hope.

I have choices that bring me joy.

The ice on the lake,

In scratched, frozen translucence,

Distorts life's image.

*I know images are not always
what they seem.*

The lake's hockey rink,

Frozen rough in real time,

Teaches needed skills.

*Unexpected challenges force
me to think differently.*

Adapting to change--

Exploring new ways to be--

I'm rich in learning.

Each change in my life
teaches me more about me.

Your anger assaults;

Accusations and demands.

I'm finding my voice.

*I learn to say what I need
you to hear.*

Winds blow; whistling through.

In empty rooms, I'm alone.

Silent peace echoes.

I find comfort and safety
in my own space.

Section 4:

Knowing Life's Beauty

Slashed by lightning's stroke,

The tree is scarred and tattered.

Still it blooms each spring.

I know, even in tragedy,
beauty and life continue.

Sun streams through crystal.

Shards of color sear my eyes,

Burning in beauty.

*I see beauty and hope
in transformation.*

Pink and blue dusk fades.

Stars, like fires in evening skies,

Light the blue-black night.

Evening brings
beauty and peace.

Tossed by endless waves,

Frosted against grains of sand,

Pebbles of sea glass.

Beauty emerges with
time and work.

I stand at the edge.

A crisp wind brushes my face--

Cheeks tingling with cold.

At the edge of tomorrow,
life exhilarates me.

Knotted red cedar

Holds the captured bird inside,

Released in carving.

*I discover strength and beauty
in unexpected places.*

Chambered nautilus--

Its life story told in the

Swirling of its shell.

*I see the beauty of life in its
patterns and shapes.*

The melon splits wide.

Sharp knife bares sweet fruit inside,

Bursting with promise.

If I look deeply enough,
I can find goodness.

Blinding white of morning

Sun reflects off snow's prisms.

Its light fills my day.

*I carry the beauty of the morning
to the work of the day.*

Sun peeks through morning.

Crystal drops of cold, wet dew

Shatter in rainbows.

Each morning brings
transformation of beauty and joy.

Silvered, shining waves,

Sparkling shades of pink and blue--

Ocean's morning light.

The beauty of reflected
light colors my day.

Section 5:

Learning My Strength

The trees sway and bend

To the music of the wind.

Season's dance of joy.

*There is joy to be found
in all seasons of life.*

Wings of gossamer--

Dragonfly hovers as still--

Paradox of strength.

*I know strength lies
in more than size.*

Cold, hard limestone shell

Shelters the soft, pink spirals.

The life inside is safe.

*My strength protects the
growing person I am.*

The storm is over.

Sun penetrates heavy clouds.

Light and warmth explode.

*I look for strength that
comes with challenges.*

Brave voice warms the dawn;

Melody of hope and light.

Spring's robins return.

*It takes courage and strength
to be among the first.*

Dropped rock stirs the lake;

Surface waves erode the shore.

Damage in small acts.

*I know even small acts
can have strong impact.*

Clouds gather, hover,

Blocking energy and light.

New winds clear the sky.

I can bring new energy and light
wherever I am.

This challenge lies broad.

I cross, one step at a time.

I will not retreat.

I overcome challenges by
taking each day as it comes.

The darkness gathers;

Night sounds—frightening, lonely.

Day will come again.

*I have faith that
I will find my way.*

Section 6:

Living and Playing

I watch the children

Laughing, circling, jumping high.

Joy shines in their eyes.

*I bring joy and playfulness
into my life every day.*

Puppies jump and play.

Flopping down, they fall asleep--

Layers of mischief.

*I embrace the playfulness
that is a part of me.*

Sun sets behind them,

The children—running, jumping--

Can't catch their shadows.

*I play with ideas
that elude me.*

Roses raise pink faces

To celebrate the sun's warmth--

Air scented with joy.

I celebrate the ambiance of joy.

Juicy strawberries

Chubby hands search tangled vines,

Cheeks covered with stains.

Even in service I find fun.

Section 7:

Seeing Tomorrow's Promise

Horizons of storms—

Clouds and wind grow miles away.

Rain's scent on the breeze.

*I am alert to my future's
potential and promise.*

The pictures I see

As I consider choices—

A collage of hope.

*I see hope in the choices
I create for myself.*

Cushioned branches of

Palest greens and newest shoots--

Spring slides to summer.

I see the promise of good
in the world around me.

Shades from blues to grays—

Adding a bare touch of pink,

Night at a distance.

Changes I see now alert
me to a different future.

Time passes quickly.

Butterflies last one season.

Lifetimes in a glance.

I celebrate each day
I am given in this life.

With held breath I wait--

First robin's song splits the air,

Fires my hope for spring.

Even when I am cold and alone,
I know there is hope.

The quiet of morning

Weaves a cocoon of peace

To wear through the day.

*I face tomorrow's challenges
with peace I find today.*

My granddaughter's voice

Holds tomorrow's poetry

In her lisping lilt.

I listen for the truth
in the voices of youth.

As snows start to melt,

Green shoots bring new promises

Of summer's lushness.

I look for signs of tomorrow's
life in today's world.

Darkening gray skies

Foreshadowing snow and ice,

Winter's storm unleashed.

*I look to today to prepare
for tomorrow's challenges.*

Section 8:

Seeking Wisdom

Before I see the beach

It's there...salty, pungent, sharp...

Scent of water's life.

*I sense new ideas and possibilities
in my surroundings.*

Stars that shine on me

Have seen the history of life.

I have much to learn.

*I see wisdom in my world,
learning from others.*

The shell at my ear

Roars with the echo of waves.

I learn old secrets.

I know the wisdom of today
lies in memories of the past.

Dark, electric sky

Lights the landscape before me.

My world becomes clear.

*I look for and learn
from flashes of insights.*

Thunder shakes the ground.

The wind bends the trees at will.

Storms cleanse the forest.

I learn from the challenges I face.

Shadowed on pink sky

Silhouette of dark mesa

Stirs tribal music.

*I learn from history in all
that is around me.*

Winds build cloud towers

Hot turbulence swirls the air.

Storms scour my valley.

I look for the value in turbulence.

Building the home nests;

Finding food; raising the pups;

Knowing in the bones.

I trust the knowing
that comes with life.

Cubs tumble and fight,

They stalk, jump, and growl aloud.

Life skills learned in play.

I learn from play.

Lake's surface of glass,

Hiding turbulent patterns,

Mirrors scenes above.

I look past the surface
to see the truth beyond.